Rain

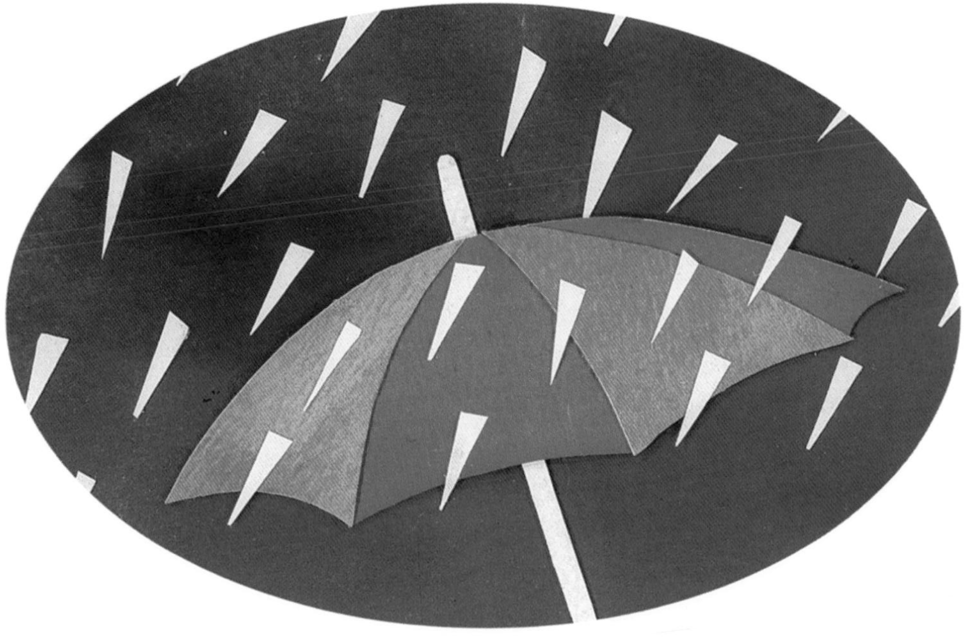

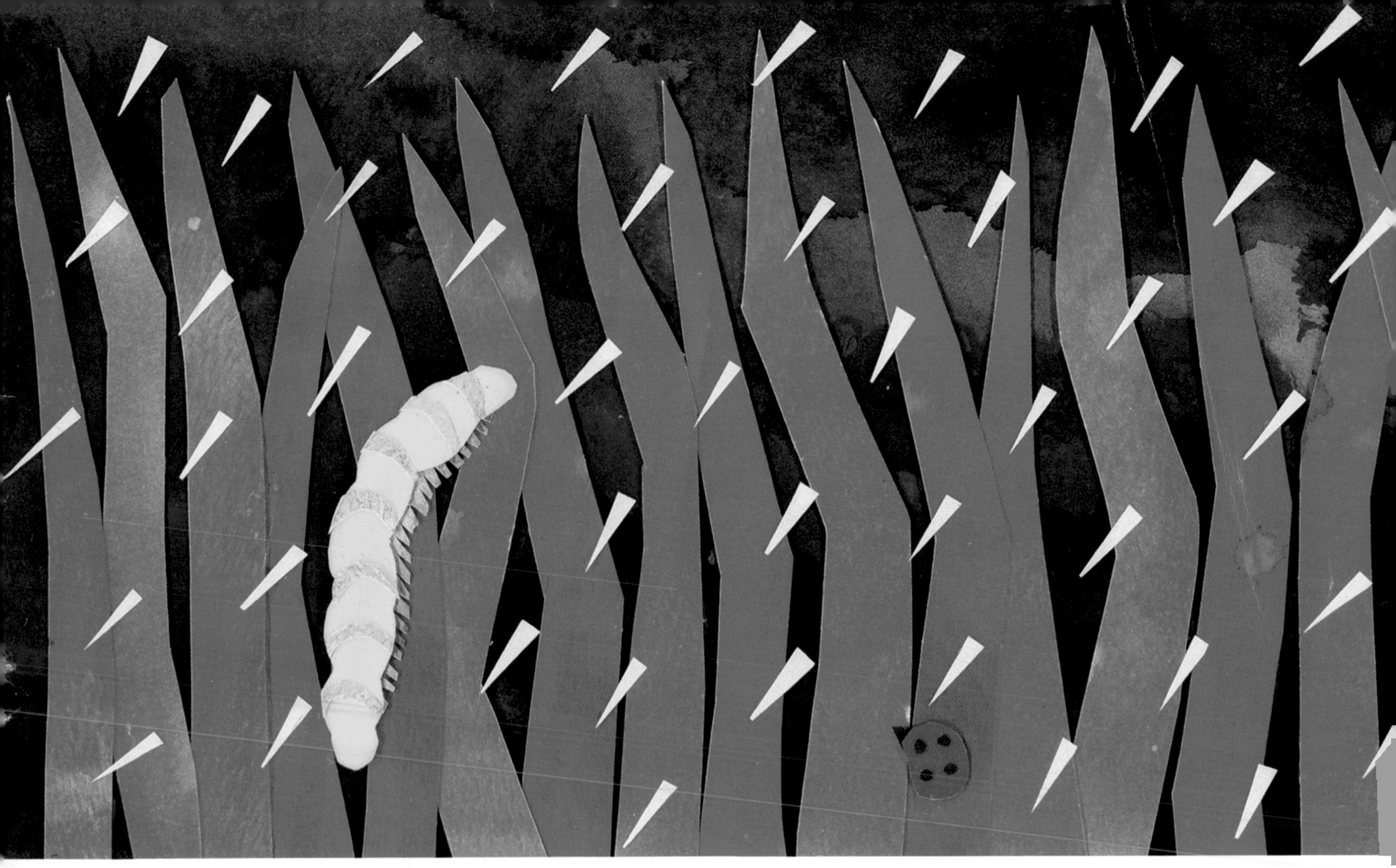

Rain on the green grass,

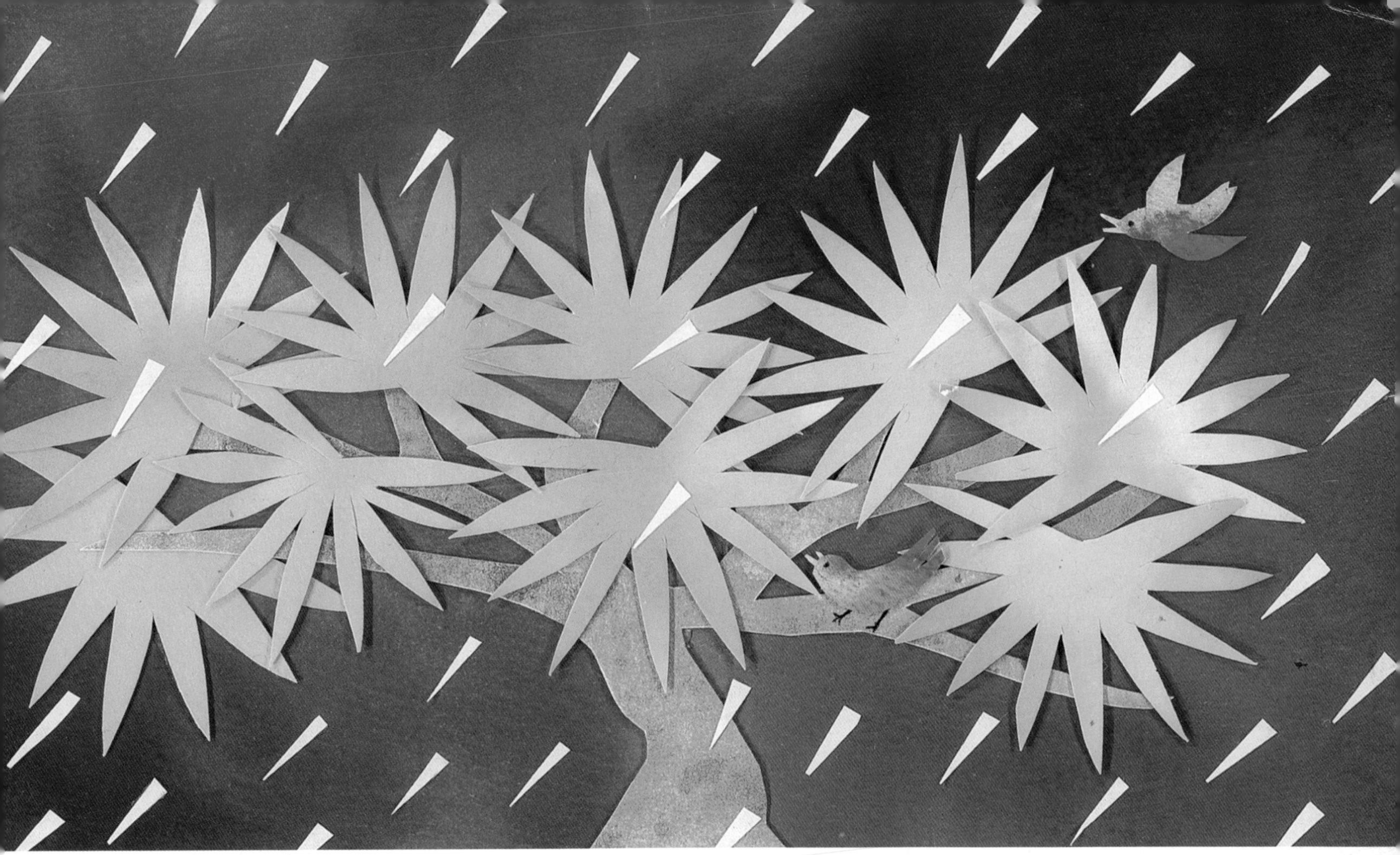

Rain on the tree,

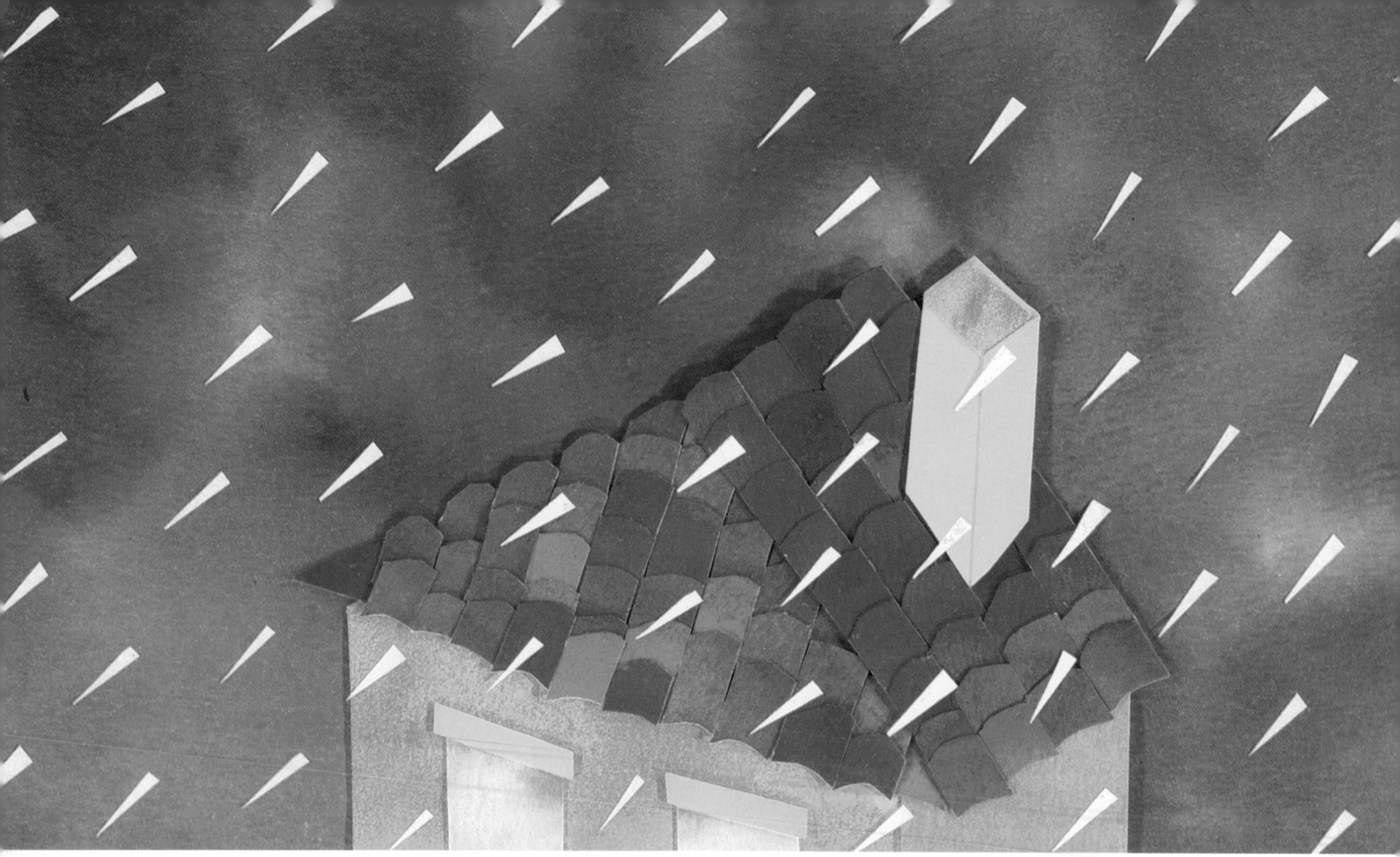

Rain on the rooftop,

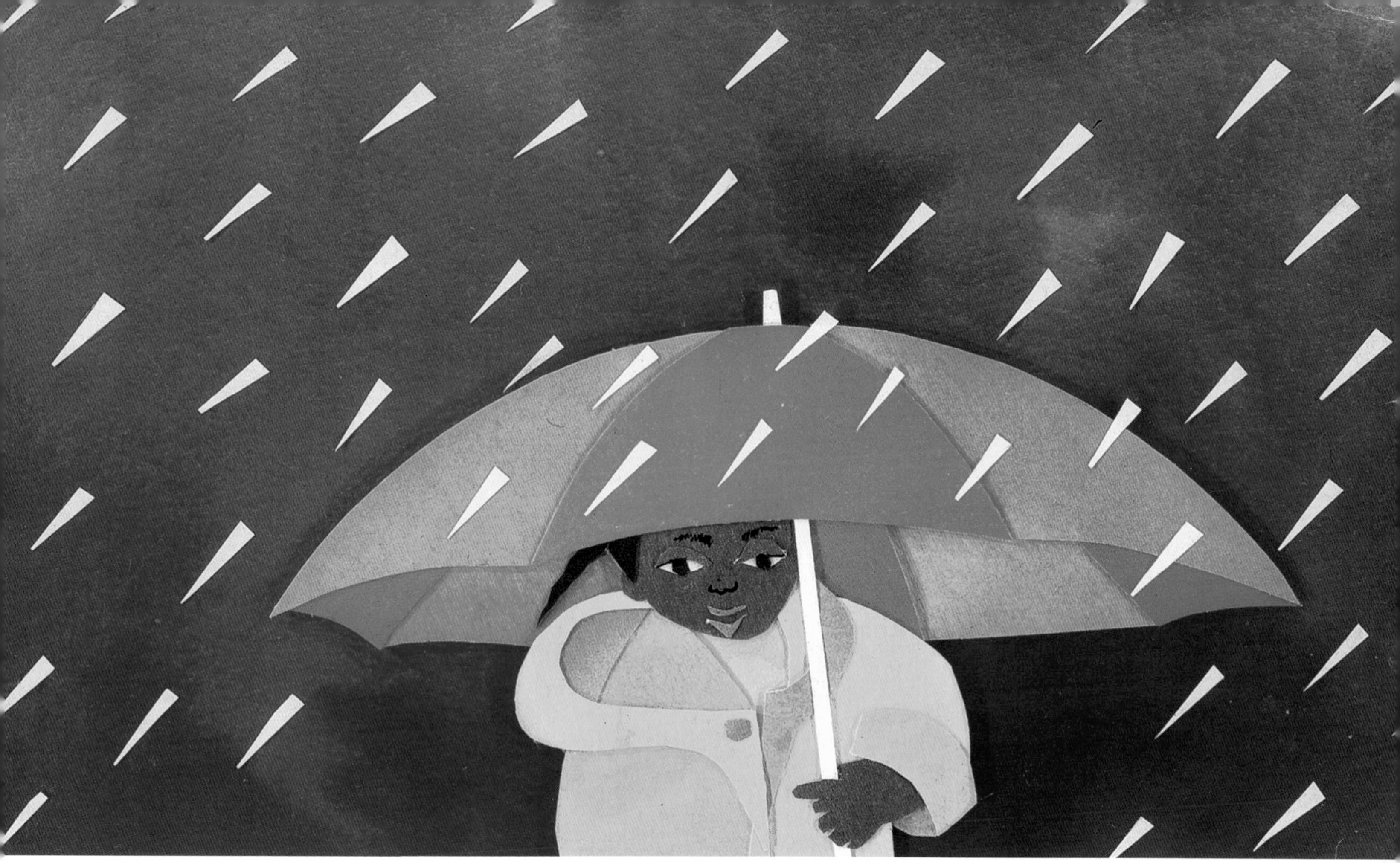

But not on me!

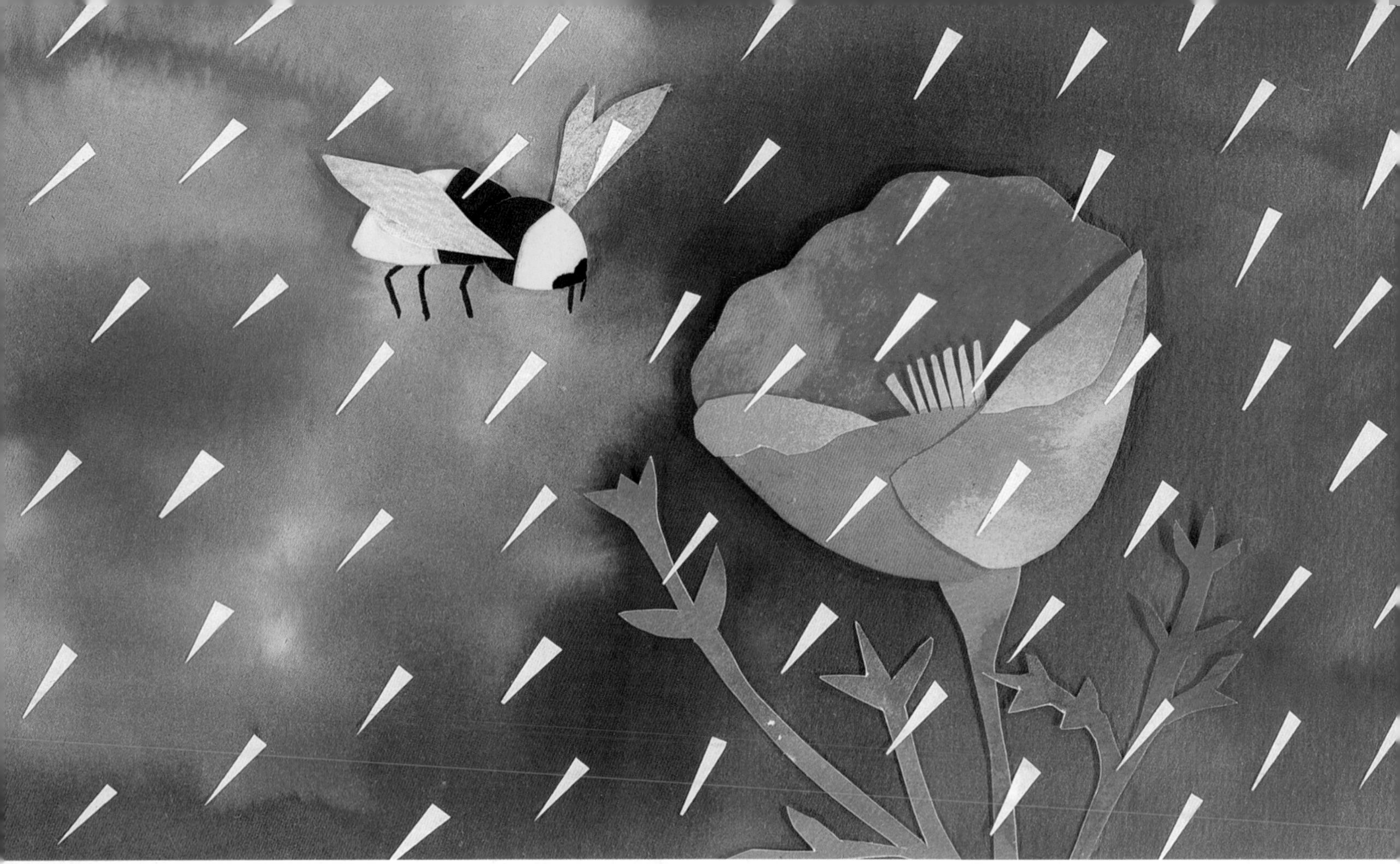

Rain on the flower,
Rain on the bee,

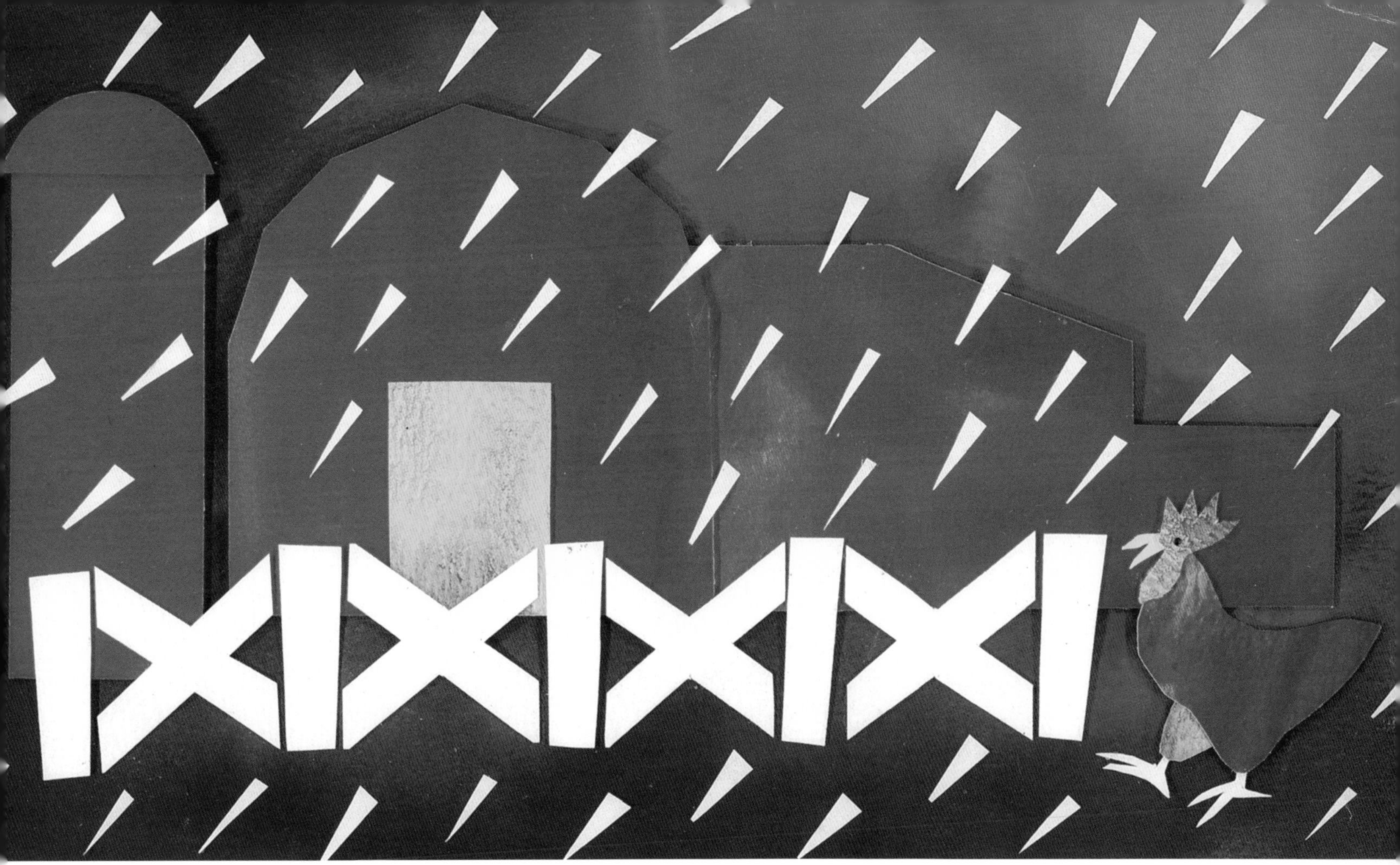

Rain on the red barn,

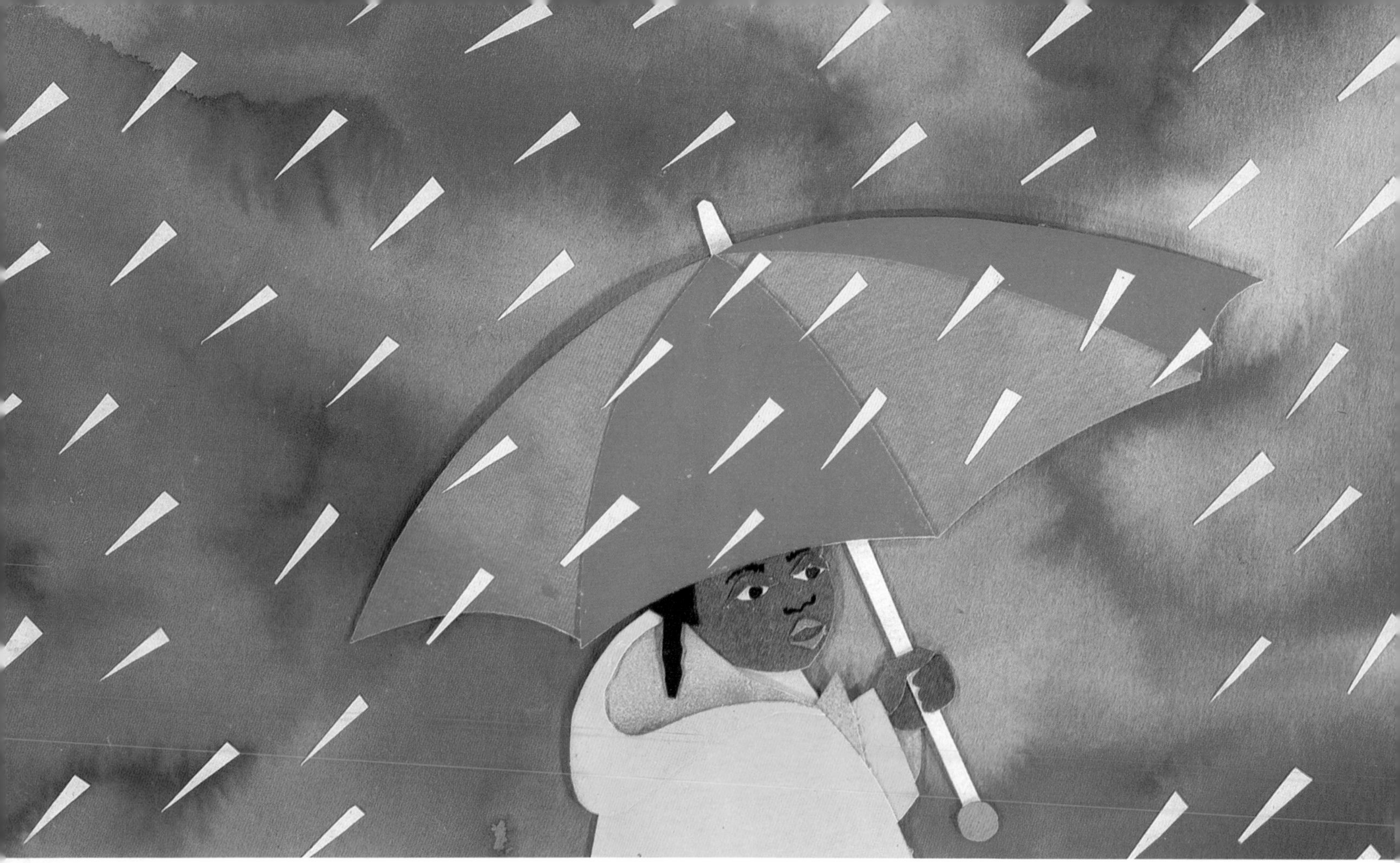

But not on me!